MW01442521

BREATHE!

Help Abby work through anxiety

© 2024 by Kaitlyn Craig
All rights reserved
ISBN: 9798321526408

Hi, I'm Abby. Im a pretty normal monster, but some things make me anxious

A few things that make me anxious are...

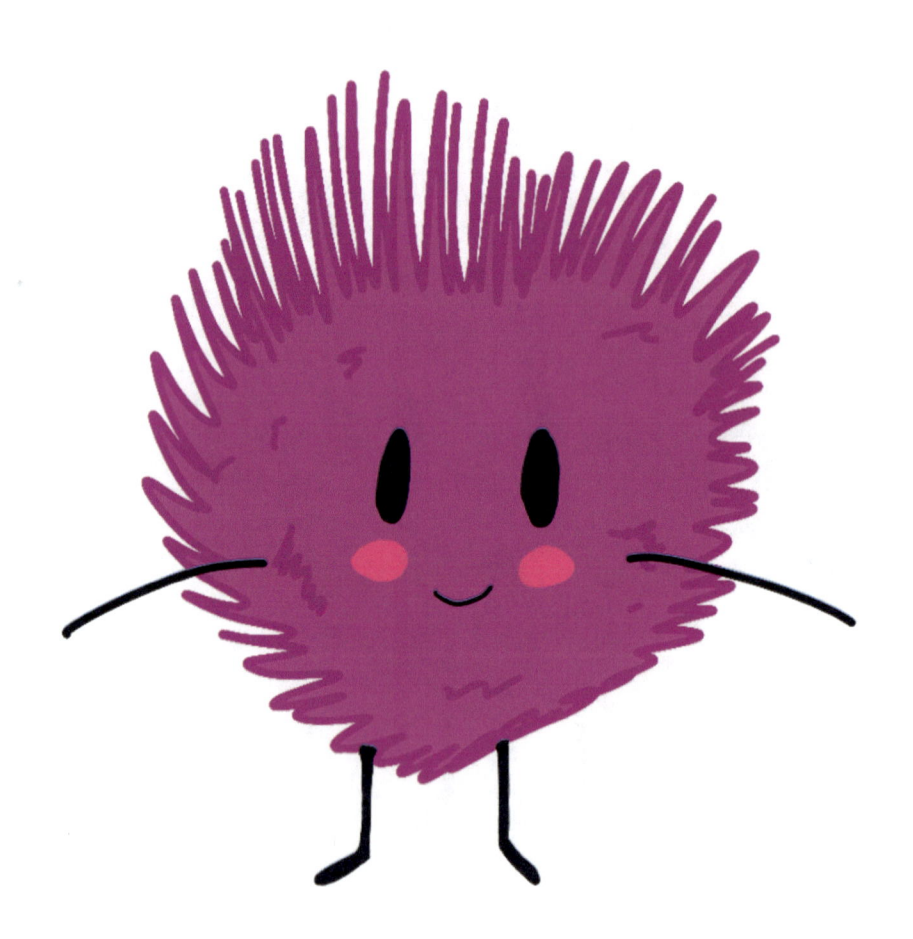

CROWDS

ATTENTION

NOISE

BARK BARK BARK

QUESTIONS

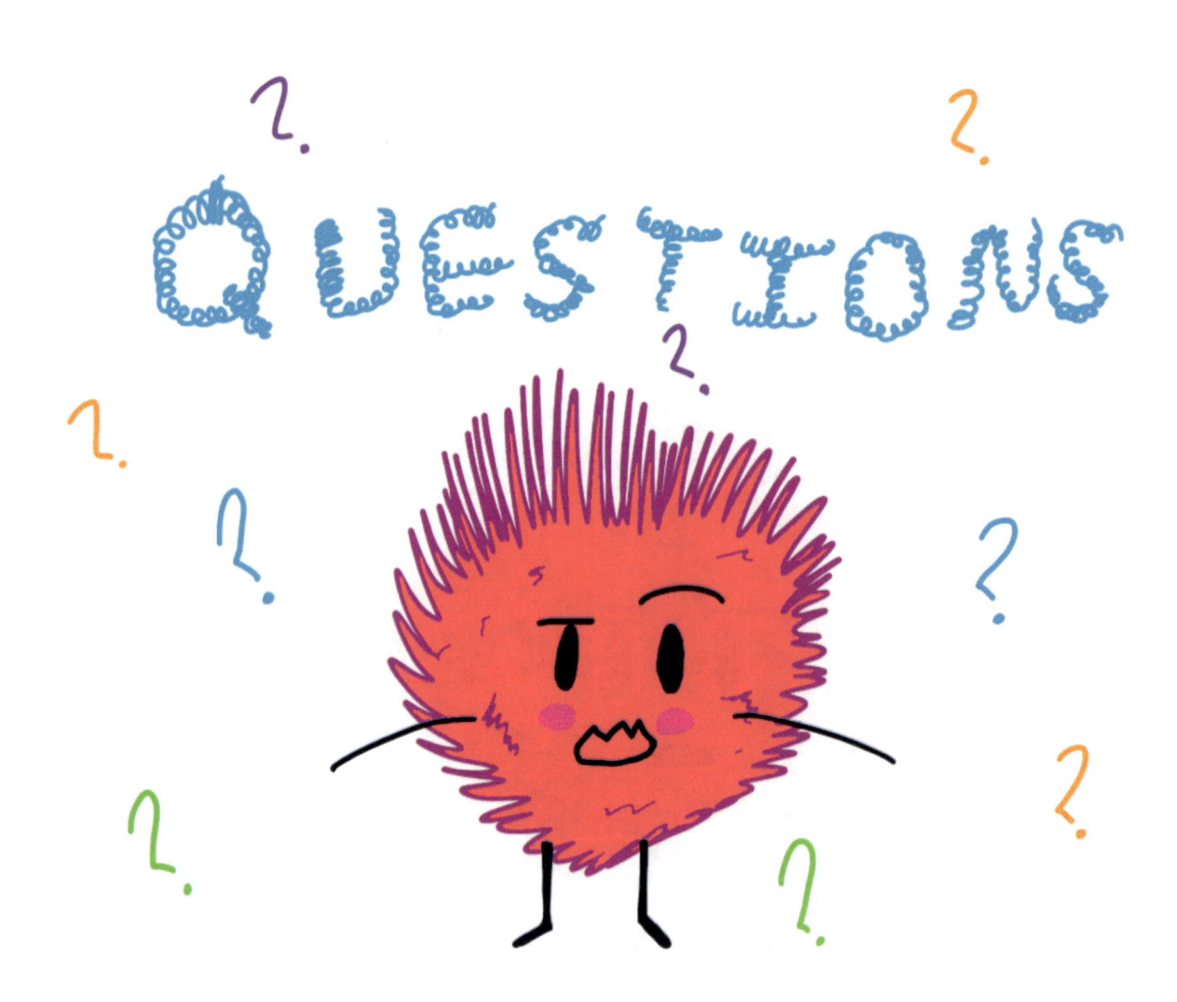

GUILT

Disappointing others

FRUSTRATION

FEARS

And...

DECISIONS

GUM?

CAKE?

Luckily, I have a way to cope with my anxiety.

I hold one hand up, fingers wide. I use my pointer finger from the other hand to trace around the outside of my hand. When my finger traces up, I breathe in. I pause at the fingertip, then breathe out as I trace down the finger. This helps me to breathe calmly and at a normal rate.

BREATHE WITH ME

Pause

Breathe out

Breathe in

Breathe out

Slowly trace my fingers and take deep breaths in and out with me!

I FEEL...

BETTER!

Oh no...

ATTENTION

BREATHE WITH ME!

Pause

Breathe out

Breathe in

Breathe out

Slowly trace my fingers and take deep breaths in and out with me!

I FEEL BETTER!

Oh no...

NOISE

BARK BARK BARK

Uh-oh, lets **BREATHE**

BARK BARK BARK

Pause

Breathe out

Breathe in

Breathe out

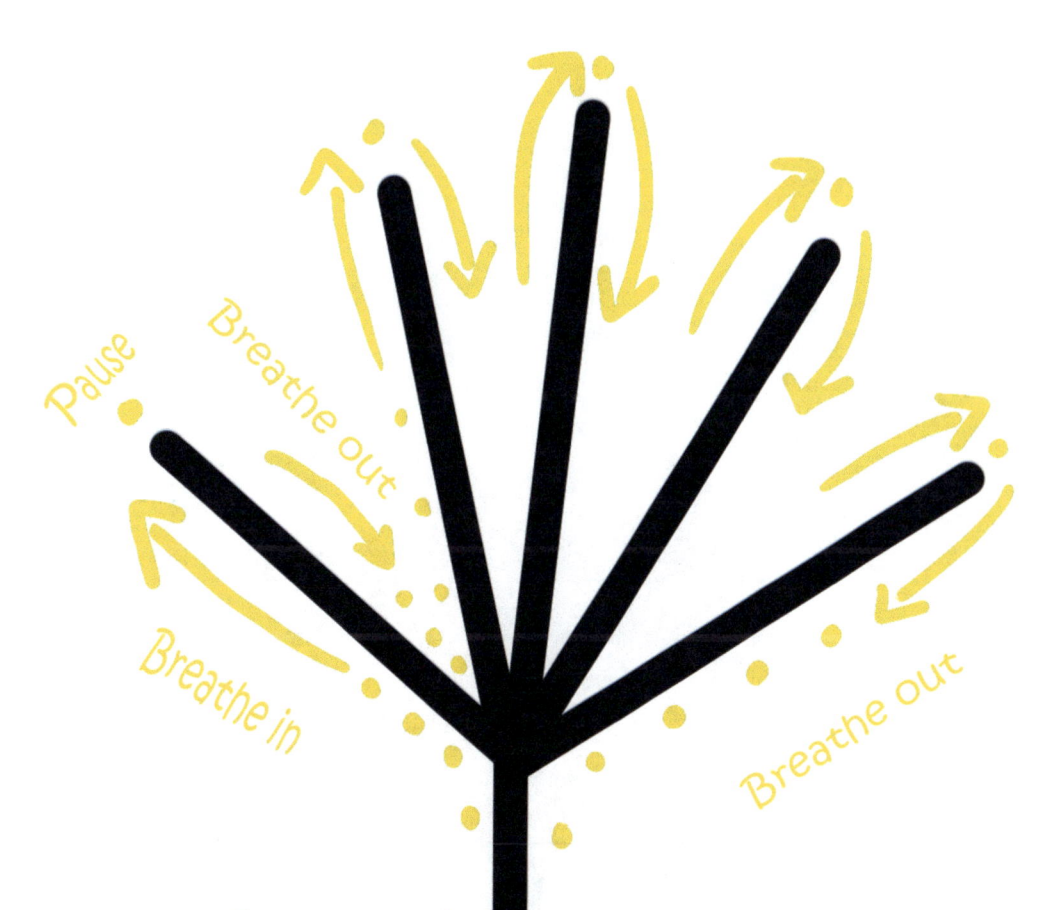

Slowly trace my fingers and take deep breaths in and out with me!

Phew...

I FEEL BETTER!

BARK BARK BARK

Ugh, not **QUESTIONS**

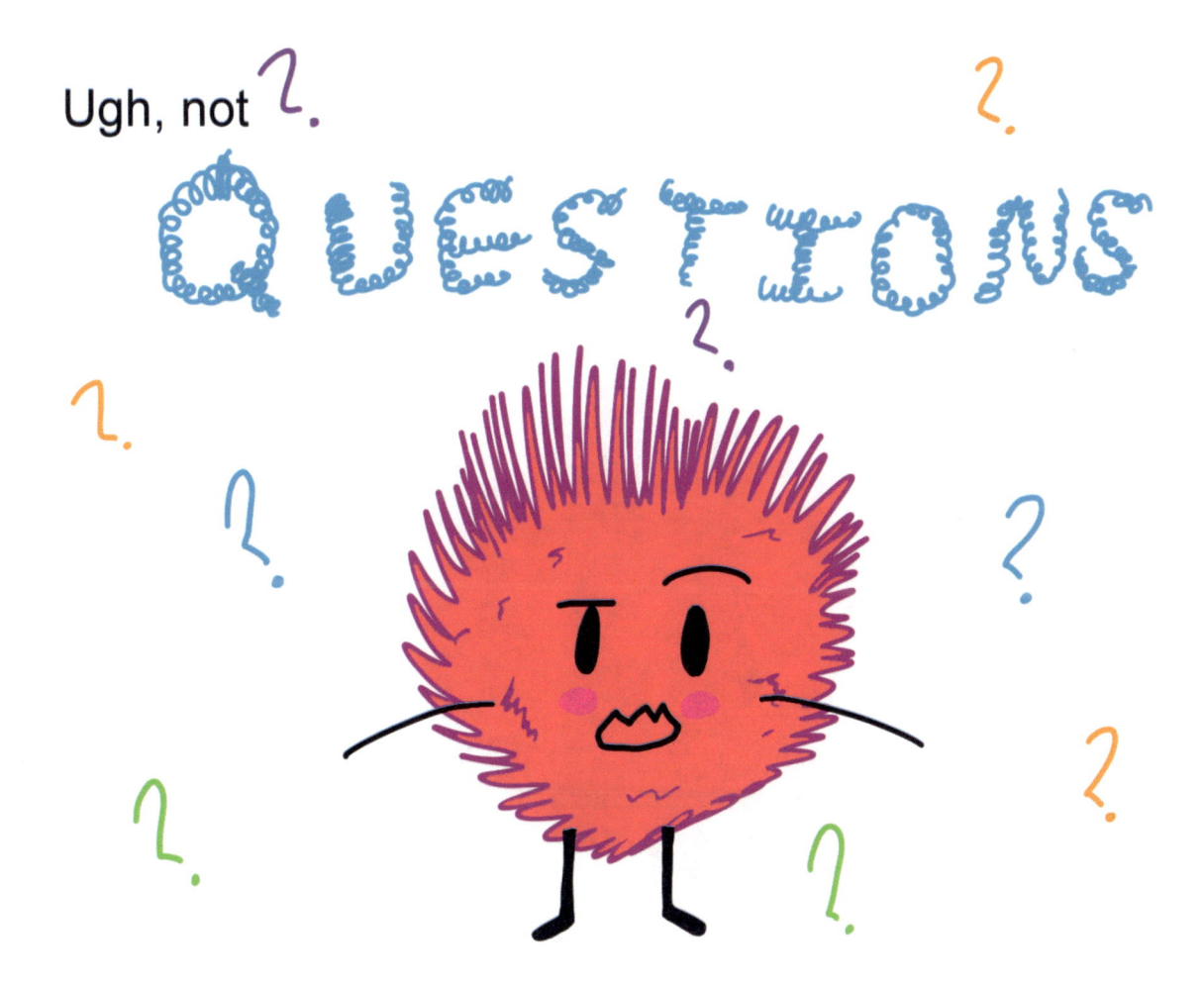

BREATHE WITH ME

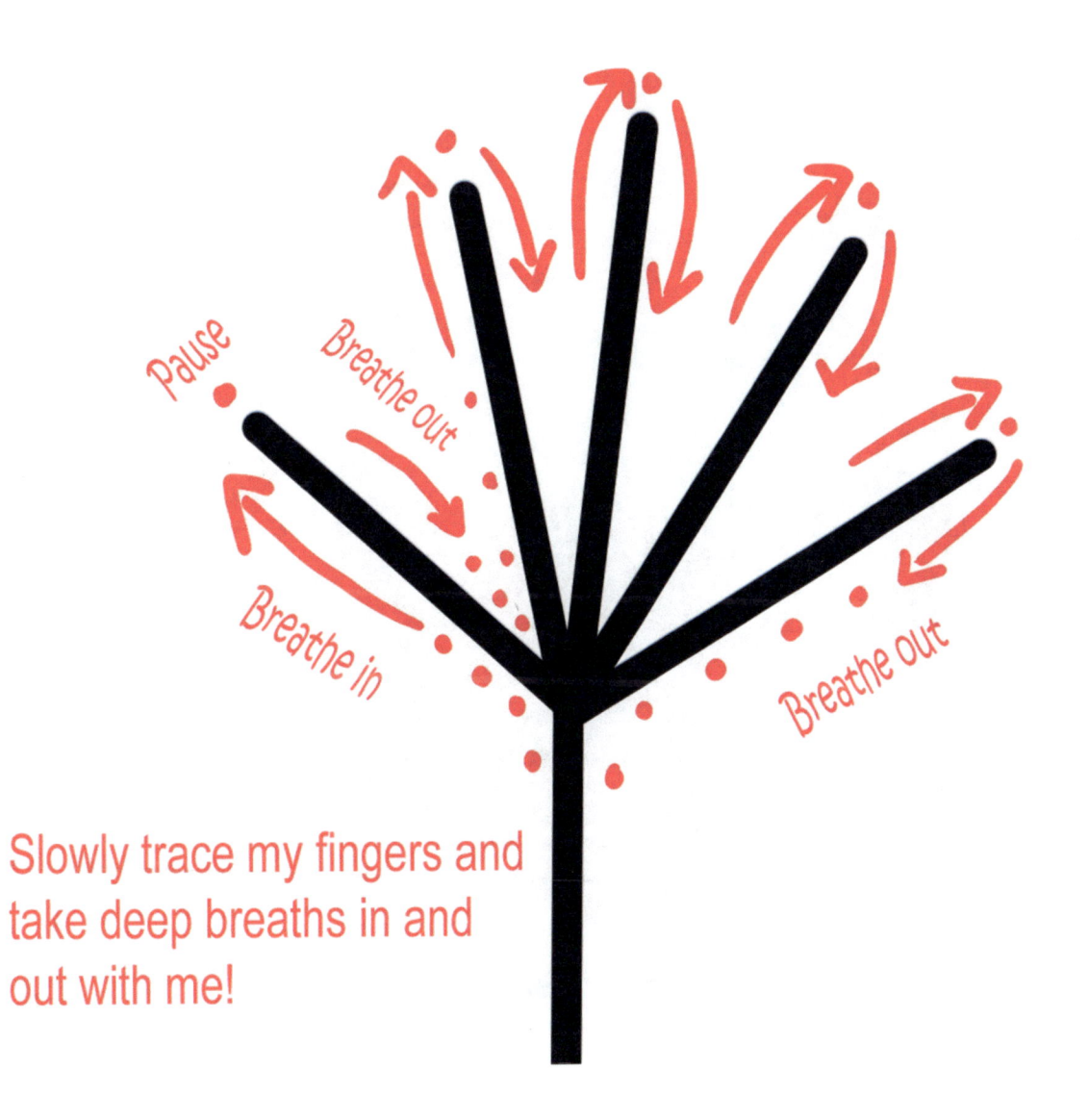

Pause

Breathe out

Breathe in

Breathe out

Slowly trace my fingers and take deep breaths in and out with me!

I FEEL BETTER!

Oh no! Now I feel

GUILT

Disappointing others

BREATHE WITH ME!

Disappointing others

Pause • Breathe out • Breathe in • Breathe out

Slowly trace my fingers and take deep breaths in and out with me!

I FEEL BETTER!

Oh no...

FRUSTRATION

BREATHE WITH ME

Pause

Breathe out

Breathe in

Breathe out

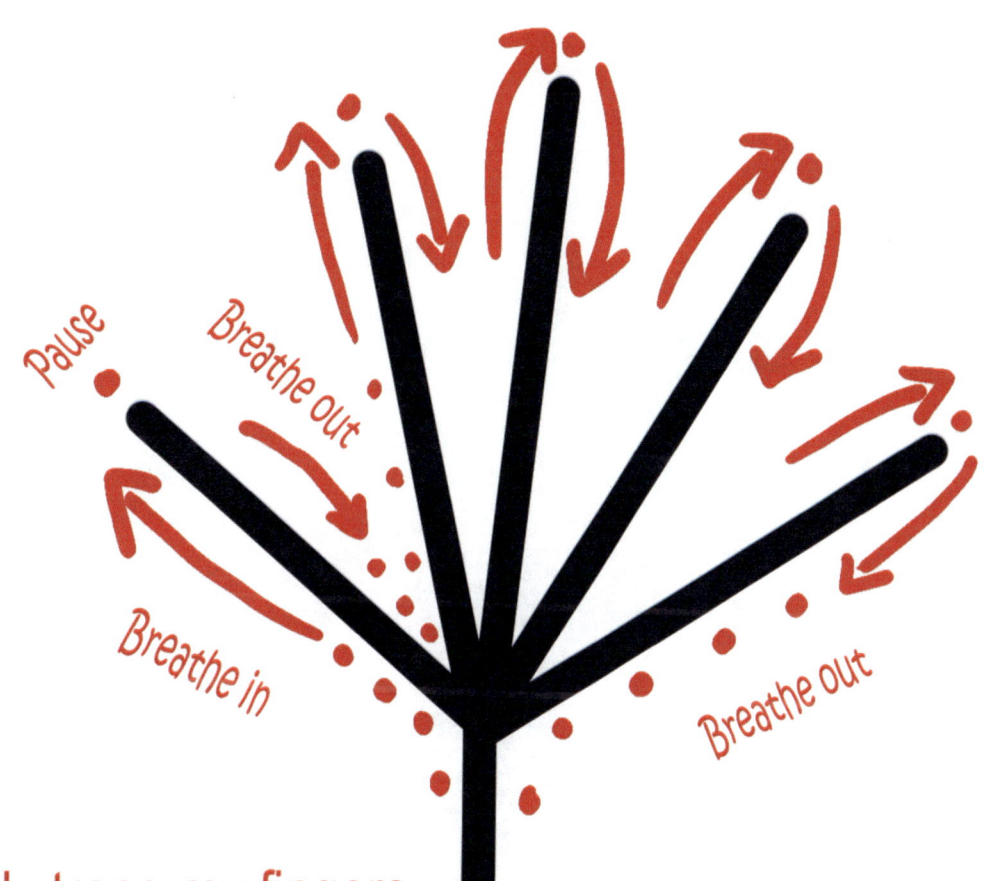

Slowly trace my fingers and take deep breaths in and out with me!

I FEEL BETTER

Oh no... **FEARS**

BREATHE WITH ME

Pause

Breathe out

Breathe in

Breathe out

Slowly trace my fingers and take deep breaths in and out with me!

I FEEL BETTER

Uh-oh... DECISIONS

GUM?

CAKE?

Pause

Breathe out

Breathe in

Breathe out

Slowly trace my fingers and take deep breaths in and out with me!

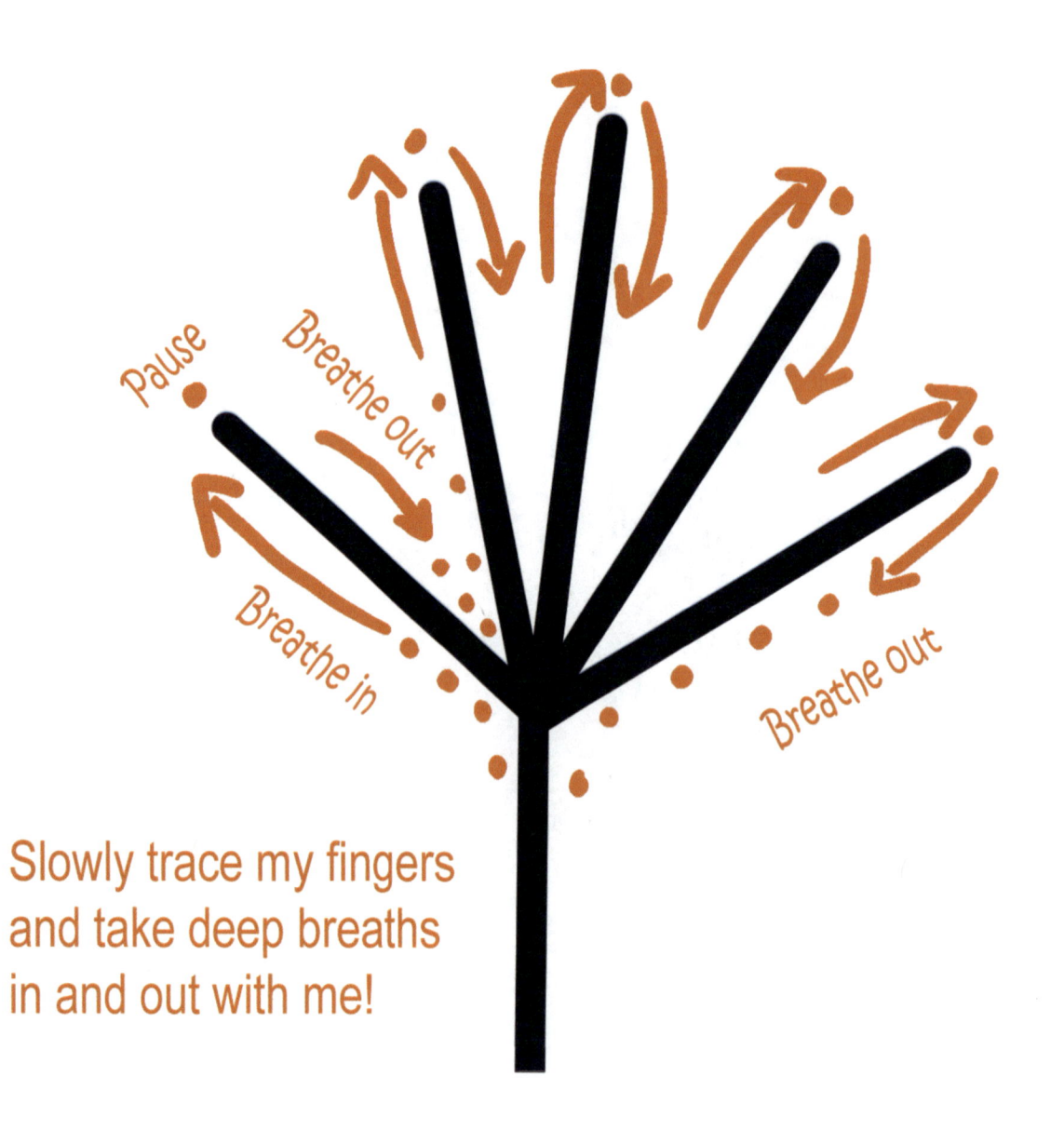

I FEEL BETTER!

Gum?

Cake?

Thank you for helping me through my anxiety! Maybe you can try breathing and tracing your fingers when you feel anxious too!

Made in the USA
Columbia, SC
18 July 2024